To Linda —
Who loves all things large & small
All things bright & beautiful —
Al & Kay

1981
The Best!

The Beauty of Birds

With Original Paintings by Wayne Trimm

Poetry selected by J. W. Dunn

Published by The C. R. Gibson Company
Norwalk, Connecticut

Copyright© MCMLXXIV by
The C. R. Gibson Company, Norwalk, Connecticut
All rights reserved
Printed in the United States of America
Library of Congress Catalog Card Number: 73-88088
ISBN: 0-8378-1864-8

Contents

Yellow-shafted Flicker The Woodpecker by Elizabeth Madox Roberts 5

The Barn Swallow The Swallows by Andrew Young 7

The Chickadee The Chickadee by Ralph Waldo Emerson
   I Heard a Bird Sing by Oliver Herford 9

Ruby-throated Hummingbird Hummingbird by D. H. Lawrence 11

Bluebird Bluebird, What Do You Feed On? by Carl Sandburg 13

The Water Ousel The Water Ousel by Mary Webb 15

Snowy Owl When Cats Run Home by Alfred, Lord Tennyson 17

Goldfinch Goldfinches by John Keats
   A Nest In The Sun by James Russell Lowell 19

Redwing Blackbird Redwings by Ruby Zagoren
   Hallmarks by Patricia Bever 21

Blue Jays Blue Jay by Patricia Bever 23

Skylark To a Skylark by Percy Bysshe Shelley 25

Bluethroat The Thrush's Nest by John Clare 27

Cardinal Cardinal by Ruby Zagoren 29

American Eagle Eagles by Vasily Bashkin 31

Nightingales Nightingales by Robert Bridges 33

Snowy Egrets Egrets by Judith Wright 35

Pale-breasted Spinetail The Oven Bird by Robert Frost 37

The Sandhill Crane The Sandhill Crane by Mary Austin 39

Yellow-shafted Flicker

The Woodpecker

The woodpecker pecked out a little round hole
And made him a house in the telephone pole.

One day when I watched he poked out his head,
And he had on a hood and a collar of red.

When the streams of rain pour out of the sky,
And the sparkles of lightning go flashing by,

And the big, big wheels of thunder roll,
He can snuggle back in the telephone pole.

ELIZABETH MADOX ROBERTS

Barn Swallows

The Swallows

All day—when early morning shone
With every dewdrop its own dawn
And when cockchafers were abroad
Hurtling like missiles that had lost their road—

The swallows twisting here and there
Round unseen corners of the air
Upstream and down so quickly passed
I wondered that their shadows flew as fast.

They steeple-chased over the bridge
And dropped down to a drowning midge
Sharing the river with the fish,
Although the air itself was their chief dish.

Blue-winged snowballs! until they turned
And then with ruddy breasts they burned;
All in one instant everywhere,
Jugglers with their own bodies in the air.

ANDREW YOUNG

Chickadee

The Chickadee

Piped a tiny voice hard by,
Gay and polite, a cheerful cry,
"Chic-chicadee-dee!" Saucy note
Out of a sound heart and a merry throat,
As if it said, "Good day, good sir.
Fine afternoon, old passenger!
Happy to meet you in these places
When January brings new faces!"

RALPH WALDO EMERSON

I Heard a Bird Sing

I heard a bird sing
In the dark of December
A magical thing
And sweet to remember.

"We are nearer to Spring
Than we were in September,"
I heard a bird sing
In the dark of December.

OLIVER HERFORD

Ruby-throated Hummingbird

Hummingbird

*I can imagine, in some otherworld
Primeval-dumb, far back
In that most awful stillness, that only gasped and
    hummed,
Hummingbirds raced down the avenues.*

*Before anything had a soul,
While life was a heave of Matter, half inanimate,
This little bit chipped off in brilliance
And went whizzing through the slow, vast, succulent
    stems.*

*I believe there were no flowers then,
In the world where the hummingbird flashed ahead of
    creation.
I believe he pierced the slow vegetable veins with his
    long beak.
Probably he was big
As mosses, and little lizards, they say, were once big.
Probably he was a jabbing, terrifying monster.*

*We look at him through the wrong end of the long tele-
    scope of Time,
Luckily for us.*

                                                    D. H. LAWRENCE

Bluebird

Bluebird What Do You Feed On?

Bluebird, what do you feed on?
It is true you gobble up worms, you
  swallow bugs,
And your bill picks up corn, seed,
  berries.
This is only part of the answer.
Your feathers have captured a piece of
  smooth sky.
Your wings are burnished with
  lake-morning blue.
It is not a worm blue nor a bug
  blue nor the blue
Of corn or berry you shine with.
Bluebird, we come to you for facts,
  for valuable
Information, for secret reports.
Bluebird, tell us, what do you
  feed on?

CARL SANDBURG

Water Ousel

The Water Ousel

Where on the wrinkled stream the willows lean,
And fling a very ecstacy of green
Down the dim crystal; and the chestnut tree
Admires her large-leaved shadow, swift and free,
A water-ousel came, with such a flight
As archangels might envy. Soft and bright
Upon a water-kissing bough she lit,
And washed and preened her silver breast, though it
Was dazzling fair before. Then twittering
She sang, and made obeisance to the Spring.
And in the wavering amber at her feet
Her silent shadow, with obedience meet,
Made her quick, imitative curtsies, too.
Maybe she dreamed a nest, so safe and dear,
Where the keen spray leaps whitely to the weir;
And smooth, warm eggs that hold a mystery;
And stirrings of life and twitterings, that she
Is passionately glad of; and a breast
As silver-white as hers, which without rest
Or languor, borne by spread wings swift and strong,
Shall fly upon her service all day long.
She hears a presage in the ancient thunder
Of the silken fall, and her small soul in wonder
Makes preparation as she deems most right,
Repurifying what before was white
Against the day when, like a beautiful dream,
Two little ousels shall fly with her down stream,
And even the poor, dumb shadow-bird shall flit
With two small shadows following after it.

MARY WEBB

Snowy Owl

When Cats Run Home

When cats run home and light is come,
　　And dew is cold upon the ground,
And the far-off stream is dumb,
　　And the whirring sail goes round,
　　And the whirring sail goes round;
　　　　Alone and warming his five wits,
　　　　The white owl in the belfry sits.

When merry milkmaids click the latch,
　　And rarely smells the new-mown hay,
And the cock hath sung beneath the thatch
　　Twice or thrice his roundelay,
　　Twice or thrice his roundelay;
　　　　Alone and warming his five wits,
　　　　The white owl in the belfry sits.

　　　　　　　　ALFRED, LORD TENNYSON

Goldfinch

Goldfinches

Sometimes goldfinches one by one will
   drop
From low hung branches; little space
   they stop;
But sip, and twitter, and their feathers
   sleek;
Then off at once, as in a wanton freak:
Or perhaps, to show their black, and
   golden wings,
Pausing upon their yellow flutterings.

                 JOHN KEATS

A Nest in the Sun

And there's never a leaf nor a blade too mean
To be some happy creature's palace;
The little bird sits at his door in the sun,
Atilt like a blossom among the leaves,
And lets his illumined being o'errun
With the deluge of summer it receives;
His mate feels the eggs beneath her wings,
And the heart in her dumb breast flutters and sings;
He sings to the wide world, and she to her nest,
In the nice ear of Nature which song is best?

                 JAMES RUSSELL LOWELL

Redwing Blackbird

Redwings

Where meadow bogs,
Where hummocks group,
The Redwings come—
The throaty troop.

The meadow fills
As Redwings raise
In hoarse bird trills
Their rusty praise.
   RUBY ZAGOREN

Hallmarks

Never cease to love
The little beauties God has set like gems
At the rich borders of a day.
Long liquid song of a starling
Sipping the morning through a golden straw.
Clear crisp cadence of a cardinal's call,
Splashed like ruby chips against the sky,
And the soft sigh
Of scarcely moving leaves.
 Sudden glory of a sunset,
 Quiet awareness of a star,
 Unspoken mystery of moonlight,
 Sacred, earth-sweet scent of night,
 High resonance of a cricket's music
  filing the night to smoothness—
Such are the hallmarks of Almighty God.
   PATRICIA BEVER

Blue Jay

Blue Jay

Regal and rich as a tropical butterfly
He spreads the blazing blueness of his wings,
Cresting them in classic attitude,
Takes a soft plunge in crystal syrup air
With swift nonchalance to show that, should he care,
He could stop midway and keep floating there.

He settles, near and startling, on my sill,
Cocking his head and jerking his plaid tail.
Beneath the velvet whiteness of his throat
A pulse is pounding.
From his sharp black eyes
There glows intelligence, somehow terrible.
He utters a remark, exuding overtones
Liquid as juice from the crushing of ripe fruit.
He launches himself suddenly airward
And flashes to find some errand in the trees.

If there were but a few blue jays on earth
How fortunate we should be, ever to see one!
But God is generous with such beauty.
And no one ever is heard to say, "Oh look!
A plump blue miracle has come down from the sky
One sacred moment, and is sitting here
Quite near!"

PATRICIA BEVER

Skylark

To a Skylark

Hail to thee, blithe spirit!
   Bird thou never wert,
That from Heaven, or near it,
   Pourest thy full heart
In profuse strains of unpremeditated art.

Higher still and higher
   From the earth thou springest
Like a cloud of fire;
   The blue deep thou wingest,
And singing still dost soar, and soaring
   ever singest.

In the golden lightning
   Of the sunken sun,
O'er which clouds are brightening,
   Thou dost float and run;
Like an unbodied joy whose race is just begun.

The pale purple even
   Melts around thy flight;
Like a star of heaven,
   In the broad daylight
Thou art unseen, but yet I hear thy
   shrill delight,

*   *   *

Teach me half the gladness
   That thy brain must know,
Such harmonious madness
   From my lips would flow,
The world should listen then, as I am
   listening now.

PERCY BYSSHE SHELLEY

Bluethroat

The Thrush's Nest

Within a thick and spreading hawthorn bush,
  That overhung a molehill large and round,
I heard from morn to morn a merry thrush
  Sing hymns to sunrise, and I drank the sound
With joy; and, often an intruding guest,
  I watched her secret toils from day to day,
How true she warped the moss to form a nest,
  And modelled it within with wood and clay;
And by-and-by, like heath-bells gilt with dew,
  There lay her shining eggs, as bright as flowers,
Ink-spotted-over shells of greeny blue;
  And there I witnessed, in the sunny hours,
    A brood of nature's minstrels chirp and fly,
    Glad as that sunshine and the laughing sky.

JOHN CLARE

Cardinals

Cardinal

I never knew that fire could fly
Or drop like a comet down from the sky
Or one red bird could brighten the day
With a flash of wings along the way.

I didn't know his voice could bring
The spheres to earth when he started to sing.
Yet when this bird sang from a tree,
I knew he was singing just for me.

RUBY ZAGOREN

American Eagle

Eagles

Upon the black brow of a cliff where no life ever stirred
Alighted strong, hoary-winged eagles, grave bird upon bird.

They whetted their claws on the rock, sitting massive and glum
And loudly they called on their lately-fledged comrades to come.

How sure was the beat of their great heavy wings on the skies;
A furious strength was ablaze in their obdurate eyes.

To each new arrival their welcome was savagely clear:
"Hail, comrade! Delay not! The days we have longed for are near!"

VASILY BASHKIN

(*Translated from the Russian by Babette Deutsch*)

Nightingale

Nightingales

Beautiful must be the mountains whence ye come,
And bright in the fruitful valleys the streams wherefrom
    Ye learn your song:
Where are those starry woods? O might I wander there,
   Among the flowers, which in that heavenly air
    Bloom the year long!

Nay, barren are those mountains and spent the streams:
Our song is the voice of desire, that haunts our dreams,
    A throe of the heart,
Whose pining visions dim, forbidden hopes profound,
   No dying cadence nor long sigh can sound,
    For all our art.

Alone, aloud in the raptured ear of men
We pour our dark nocturnal secret; and then,
    As night is withdrawn
From these sweet-springing meads and bursting boughs of May,
   Dream, while the innumerable choir of day
    Welcome the dawn.

                                        ROBERT BRIDGES

Snowy Egret

Egrets

*Once as I travelled through a quiet evening,
I saw a pool, jet-black and mirror still.
Beyond, the slender paperbacks stood crowding;
each on its own white image looked its fill,
and nothing moved but thirty egrets wading—
thirty egrets in a quiet evening.*

*Once in a lifetime, lovely past believing,
your lucky eyes may light on such a pool.
As though for many years I had been waiting,
I watched in silence, till my heart was full
of clear dark water, and white trees unmoving,
and, whiter yet, those egrets wading.*

JUDITH WRIGHT

Pale-breasted Spinetail

The Oven Bird

There is a singer everyone has heard,
Loud, a mid-summer and a mid-wood bird,
Who makes the solid tree trunks sound again.
He says that leaves are old and that for flowers
Mid-summer is to spring as one to ten.
He says the early petal-fall is past
When pear and cherry bloom went down in showers
On sunny days a moment overcast;
And comes that other fall we name the fall.
He says the highway dust is over all.
The bird would cease and be as other birds
But that he knows in singing not to sing.
The question that he frames in all but words
Is what to make of a diminished thing.

ROBERT FROST

Sandhill Crane

The Sandhill Crane

*Whenever the days are cool and clear
The sandhill crane goes walking
Across the field by the flashing weir
Slowly, solemnly stalking.
The little frogs in the tules hear
And jump for their lives when he comes near,
The minnows scuttle away in fear,
When the sandhill crane goes walking.*

*The field folk know if he comes that way,
Slowly, solemnly stalking,
There is danger and death in the least delay
When the sandhill crane goes walking.
The chipmunks stop in the midst of their play,
The gophers hide in their holes away
And hush, oh, hush! the field mice say,
When the sandhill crane goes walking.*

MARY AUSTIN

Acknowledgements

The editor and the publisher have made every effort to trace the ownership of all copyrighted material and to secure permission from copyright holders of such material. In the event of any question arising as to the use of any material the publisher and editor, while expressing regret for inadvertent error, will be pleased to make the necessary corrections in future printings. Thanks are due to the following authors, publishers, publications and agents for permission to use the material indicated.

ANGUS & ROBERTSON (U.K.) LTD., for "Egrets" from *Collected Poems 1942/70* by Judith Wright.

LEONARD CLARK, Literary Executor of The Andrew Young Estate, for "The Swallows" by Andrew Young.

HARCOURT BRACE JOVANOVICH, INC., for "Bluebird, What Do You Feed On?" from *Wind Song,* © 1960 by Carl Sandburg.

HOLT, RINEHART AND WINSTON, INC., for "The Oven Bird" from *The Poetry of Robert Frost,* edited by Edward Connery, copyright 1916, © 1969 by Holt, Rinehart and Winston, Inc., copyright 1944 by Robert Frost.

HOUGHTON MIFFLIN COMPANY, for "The Sandhill Crane" by Mary Austin, from *The Children Sing in The Far West.*

AVRAHAM YARMOLINSKY, for "Eagles" by Vasily Baskin, from *A Treasury of Russian Verse,* chosen and translated by Babette Deutsch and Avraham Yarmolinsky, copyright 1921.

Zagoren, Ruby, for "Redwings" and "Cardinal".

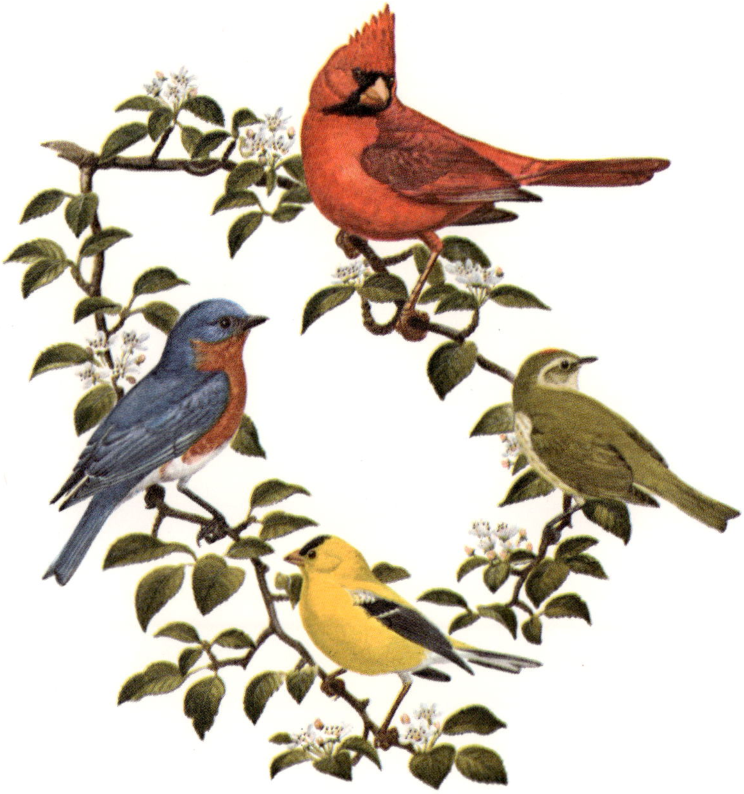